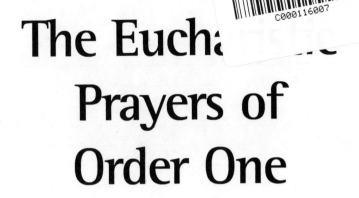

The Eucharistic Prayers of Order One

Colin Buchanan

Bishop of Woolwich

Charles Read

Lecturer in Liturgy, Cranmer Hall, Durham

GROVE BOOKS LIMITED
RIDLEY HALL RD CAMBRIDGE CB3 9HU

Contents

Acknowledgments

We are both very grateful both for the experience of living with the creation of the texts of new eucharistic prayers, and for the supportive and critical role played by our colleagues of the Group for Renewal of Worship (GROW) in the writing of this booklet. We ourselves commend related productions from the GROW team:

(a) Colin Buchanan's earlier *Eucharistic Consecration* (Grove Worship booklet W 148).

(b) Mark Earey's, *Producing your own Orders of Service* (Church House Publishing, April 2000, £7.95).

(c) Jeremy Fletcher's forthcoming *The New Eucharist: Order One* (Grove Worship booklet W 159).

(d) The major companion to Common Worship, *Common Worship Today* (HarperCollins, December 2000, 256 pp, hardback and fully illustrated, price to be announced), edited by Mark Earey and Gilly Myers with Colin Buchanan and Trevor Lloyd as consultant editors and major contributors. This gives a much fuller biblical and historical background to eucharistic liturgy in general and to Order One in particular, as well as handling each eucharistic prayer separately and looking at the celebration of the rite overall.

COB/CWR April 2000

The Cover Illustration is by Peter Ashton

First Impression June 2000

ISSN 1367-0840

ISBN 1 85174 436 3

1
Introduction

The new eucharistic Orders of the Church of England were published on 6 April 2000, in the form of a 'sample' booklet offprinted in two colours from the forthcoming Common Worship Book. By a monumental administrative achievement a copy was sent free to every known cleric in the Church of England—25,000 copies in all. The rites are only authorized from Advent Sunday (3 December) 2000, so, at the time of our writing this, they are published in order that parishes and individuals may have had a good chance to study them, and so be ready to go over to them when the rites are authorized. There is but a short overlap, for the *ASB* rites will lapse on 31 December 2000, so decisions about the new services need to be taken in good time.

The new texts comprise two 'Orders,' each with modern and antique language alternatives. Here we refer simply to the eight eucharistic prayers in Order One in modern language. The first three (labelled 'A,' 'B,' and 'C') are minor adaptations of the first, third and fourth eucharistic prayers in Rite A and receive briefer treatment, whilst prayers D to H are set out in full themselves and with a commentary on successive pages for each one. We thus discuss each one in its own right and according to its own characteristics, but neither comment here on the pros and cons of having eight, nor discuss them comparatively so as to assist a parochial choice between them. The nearest we go to comparisons is to applaud the consistent policy of Liturgical Commission, Bishops, full Synod and Revision Committees alike, that nothing should be authorized save texts which all main schools of thought can use with a good conscience. Whether that has been achieved we cannot say with absolute certainty, but it is the only policy which deserves any standing in the Church and we have good hopes it will prove to be true. The next booklet in this Grove Worship Series will be by Jeremy Fletcher and will handle the eucharistic provision overall, and questions of comparison fall more under his brief. He is a member of the Liturgical Commission and was on the Steering Committee of the General Synod's Revision Committee on the eucharistic rites.

We ourselves have stood particularly near to the eucharistic prayers and comment on them from that proximity. Colin Buchanan steered Rite A through Synod in 1979, was on the Revision Committee for the stillborn 1996 set, and, as a member of the House of Bishops, combed through the new set both initially and before Final Approval. He also picketed the Revision Committee by post, appeared before them twice, moved references back in full Synod at various points, and then tabled amendments at the Second Revision Stage. Charles Read as a member of the General Synod was on the Steering Committee of that Revision Committee, and took his own part in the redrafting and retouching which Revision Committees do.

2

The New Prayers: Historical Introduction

The compiling of a succession of eucharistic prayers for the Church of England has been a central task of liturgical commissions, bishops, synods (and their revision committees), parishes and individuals for the last 35 years. This Booklet deals with the latest flowering of that creativity in the shape of the eight prayers in Order One. But their roots are to be found at various points, some likely, some unlikely, within those three-and-a-half decades.

If the immediate history covers 35 years, the pre-history goes much further back. The structure of Cranmer's rite, whether in its pristine 1552 form, or in its marginally re-touched 1662 form, is one identified by the unique pattern of its sacramental section.[1] Its order went, in broad terms, like this:

(Offertory of money, with—in 1662—preparation of the Table)
Prayer for the Church Militant
Short Exhortation ('Ye that do truly…')
Confession
Absolution
Comfortable Words
    Dialogue
    Preface
    Sanctus
Prayer of Humble Access
    Prayer relating to the cross
    Petition for (receptionist) consecration ('grant that we receiving…may be partakers…')
    Narrative of institution (with—in 1662—manual acts)
Distribution
Lord's Prayer
    Prayer of Self-Oblation (one of two alternative prayers)

In this table the indented sections in bold type had previously been all together in sequence as a single prayer (with other elements also) in 1549. After 1552 a kind of Anglican memory of that 1549 'long prayer' surfaced in the Scottish rite of 1637, in the dreams of bishops in consultation in 1661, in the non-jurors of the eighteenth century, and in the Scottish and American lines of eucharistic development later in that same century. In the latter part of the nineteenth century a fascination with Roman texts led anglo-catholics to borrow the Roman Canon entire or to

---

1   For the reasons for Cranmer's structuring of the sacramental liturgy in 1552 see Colin Buchanan, *What Did Cranmer Think He Was Doing?* (Grove Liturgical Study 7, 1976).

cobble up Anglican imitations of it which nevertheless had a similar structure of 'the long prayer.'[2] It was against this background that W H Frere in 1911 suggested an 'interim' use, which would draw upon Cranmer's 1552 *wording*, but would stitch together the parts which are printed in bold in the table above to provide a single long prayer, and would consequently restructure the whole sacramental part of the rite to follow a 1549 or similar order.[3]

To lovers of 1662 this kind of suggestion was incomprehensible, but to those who thought Cranmer had distorted or mangled the eucharistic rite it came as a great relief and deliverance. When, in the immediately following years, it became necessary for a broad cross-section of the Church of England to agree a new (though alternative) 'long prayer,' Frere himself led the quest starting from this 'interim rite.'[4] By the time the 1927–28 proposals came in sight, that quest had moved away from Frere and was leading to a 'long prayer' with a 'petition for consecration' (or 'epiclesis') in an 'Eastern' position—that is, *after* the narrative of institution. Paradoxically this was beginning to alienate the very anglo-catholics who had initiated the quest (no-one else minded Cranmer's shape), as an epiclesis after the narrative virtually spells out that the reading of the narrative has *not* consecrated the elements, for consecration of them is still needed. All the traditional Roman ceremonial (including elevation, genuflection, and ringing of bells) becomes redundant and embarrassing if the words 'This is my body' and 'This is my blood' do *not* consecrate. The 1927–28 proposals were defeated, and, although many of the other services passed into (slightly irregular) use, no-one showed any desire for the eucharistic rite and its 'long prayer.' Extreme anglo-catholics used Rome entire; moderate ones might well use the 'interim rite'; all recognized that they were in a time of recovery of momentum.

Gregory Dix proved to be the mover. His emphasis on 'shape' as over against formulae, and his insistence that we are addressing a single prayer of *thanksgiving*, were, as stated in these broad terms, principles which even evangelicals could adopt. He might expound their historical outcropping or their potential future use in terms which imported all kinds of accoutrements unwelcome to evangelicals, but those starting principles in themselves were acceptable. He also had a cheerful contempt for law in relation to liturgy (his own use was fully Roman), and urged unofficial experimentation.[5] Indeed, in the years immediately following his publication of *The Shape of the Liturgy*, the liturgical committee of the Church of South India, far from being of his theological persuasion and working in a Church

2   See J Mark, M Dalby, *Anglican Missals and their Canons* (Alcuin/GROW Joint Liturgical Study 41, 1998).
3   W H Frere, *Some Principles of Liturgical Reform* (John Murray, 1911) pp186–194. It was not universally admired even by anglo-catholics, and Gregory Dix dismissed it with 'If you share his [Cranmer's] theology, you had much better use his liturgy as he left it, for a better expression of that theology will not be achieved by tinkering with his rite. If you do not share his theology, you will not achieve the expression of a different doctrine merely by shuffling the parts of his rite...' (*The Shape of the Liturgy*, p 692, note 1). This quotation is without prejudice to the question as to whether Dix had understood or stated Cranmer's theology fairly himself...
4   See, *eg*, G J Cuming, *A History of Anglican Liturgy* (2nd ed, MacMillan, 1982) pp166ff.
5   G Dix, *The Shape of the Liturgy* (Dacre/Black, 1945) pp 720–723.

the very existence of which he opposed and denounced, provided the first rite ever to follow out his principles and to provide a 'long prayer' which did not offend protestant and evangelical scruples. This was accepted in their Synod in 1950 and became a vital milestone put down.

In England in the 1950s much of the thrust of Dix was also taken up. In relation to the eucharistic prayer it became usual, for instance, to refer not to 'the prayer of consecration' but to 'giving thanks over the bread and wine.' In fact the presuppositions of both Dix and his contemporaries were far more strongly anglo-catholic than the innocent words 'giving thanks' might suggest; and in any case evangelicals were both weak in numbers and strong, almost Pavlovian, in reaction against any proposed revision of the Communion service. Dix himself died in 1952, but the anglo-catholic hegemony ran on, and his followers (notably in the persons of Ratcliff and Couratin) were developing in an anti-evangelical direction (and Couratin was smoothly telling evangelicals that, as they already had 1662 and were clearly never going to stir from it, they must be understanding of a catholic tendency in any new eucharistic prayer being written).[6]

Such was the background when, in the years 1963–64, Couratin began drafting on behalf of the Commission a eucharistic prayer for the rite that would in due course become Series 2. Because he persuaded the Commission that Hippolytus should be the model, he was able to write an anamnesis paragraph which stated that, in obedience to our Lord's command, we offer to God the bread and the wine. Colin Buchanan dissented; the Convocations sought first a compromise and then alternatives; the House of Laity refused alternatives and insisted on an agreed way forward; and the amended Series 2 then said, like 1549, that, to obey Christ's command to 'do this,' 'we make the memorial' of his mighty acts. The issue of which verb should be used in this paragraph, in order to state what we 'do' in commemoration of Christ, took centre stage in the years from 1966 to 1980. But meantime a text was found which most main groupings in the Church of England could use; and, poignantly, at the point of authorization of this 'Series 2' in Summer 1967, Ratcliff died suddenly and Couratin resigned from the Commission, and the theological balance and internal dynamics of the people drafting new texts changed.

In 1971 the Commission produced a revised text which, after going through Synod between November 1971 and November 1972, became the Series 3 rite which ran until 1980. The anamnesis had again attracted close attention and much energy, and gave more scope to evangelical concern to emphasize the close connection between the sacrifice of Christ on the cross and the celebration of the Supper. The Archbishops wrote that they were delighted (and perhaps they were also surprised) that a single text had been agreed. The resultant anamnesis ran:

Therefore, heavenly Father, with this bread and this cup we do this in remembrance of him: we celebrate and proclaim his perfect sacrifice made once for

---

6   According to personal conversations between Colin Buchanan and Arthur Couratin in the years 1964-67.

all upon the cross, his resurrection from the dead, and his ascension into heaven; and we look for his coming in glory.'

Series 3 in turn became the text which was to be re-touched for the *ASB*, and its anamnesis was marginally redrafted for that. However, by 1977-78 the agenda was changing. With one secure text in place, the question was whether others could be deployed as well. Series 2 usage had run on (partly because it was still in 'thou' form of address to God, whilst Series 3 was in 'you' form) and had in 1976 been incorporated with the Series 1 text (the 'Interim Rite' retouched in 1966 for authorization) into 'Series 1 and 2 Revised.'[7] So the eucharistic prayers of both these sources were now put into 'you' form and became the Second Eucharistic Prayer (from Series 2) and the Fourth (from Series 1). What then was the Third? That arose not from the Commission, but from Brian Brindley who brought to the Revision Committee (with the support of Roger Beckwith) a version of Roman Catholic Prayer II, itself drawn from Hippolytus—and it was re-touched and authorized in Rite A and has put up much mileage since.[8] The Commission had originally tried a range of other ideas on the House of Bishops, including a highly responsive prayer, but the bishops would not support these risky ventures.[9]

In the two decades since the *ASB* there has been a curious history. The Commission took seriously the call for materials for Urban Priority Areas,[10] and produced some very flexible eucharistic prayers (one of them simply a matrix) in 'Rite C' in the original *Patterns for Worship*.[11] The House of Bishops was again unadventurous and, after giving grudging encouragement to the Commission to fine-tune these prayers, then kicked them all back as unacceptable in January 1992. The Commission and House of Bishops then went through a slow 'after you, Cecil; no, after you, Claude' routine with the General Synod, the bishops asking the Synod if they would be ready to ask the bishops to bring forward prayers. In Summer 1994 the Synod said 'yes, and up to five';[12] the bishops in November 1994 responded by bringing a mere two; the Revision Committee in Spring 1995 stepped the numbers up to six and sent them to Synod; the Synod then brought no motions for re-committal at all in July 1995. All seemed agreed— and then all went wrong. A new Synod was elected in Autumn 1995; the bishops

---

7 Interestingly, this rite only obtained its necessary two-thirds majority in the House of Clergy in July 1976 by 105-51. Having obtained it, it went on to become 'Rite B' in the *ASB* (and be the basis upon which the Synod was able to resist the reintroduction of Series 1 in 1984) and to become the parent of other modern language eucharistic prayers—the Second and Fourth in Rite A, and Prayer C in Order One.

8 For a close comparison of texts see Colin Buchanan (ed), *The New Eucharistic Prayers of the Church of England* (Grove Liturgical Study LS20, 1979) or Colin Buchanan (ed), *Latest Anglican Liturgies 1976-1984* (SPCK/Alcuin, 1985) Appendix chart.

9 See the original report of the Liturgical Commission in 1978, *Holy Communion: Series 3 Revised* (SPCK, 1978) Introduction.

10 See *Faith in the City* (SPCK, 1985), pp 66–67, 136–7.

11 Liturgical Commission, *Patterns for Worship* (Church House Publishing, 1989); 'Rite C' eucharistic prayers are on pp 239–251. The final text of *Patterns* (Church House Publishing, 1995) was published without eucharistic rites.

12 The debates may be followed and checked in the General Synod's *Report of Proceedings* for any specified session.

divided over their own proposals; the Final Approval debate in February 1996 was a trail of heteregeneous complaints (including the sheer number of prayers); and the prayers were defeated in the House of Laity and passed into history.[13]

To achieve the 2000 deadline there then had to be haste. Prayers were published by the Liturgical Commission in 1997, and experimental use organized during Winter 1997-98. General Approval came in Synod in July 1998, and the Revision Committee this time received a weight of suggestions. The First Revision Stage came in July 1999; and the texts were re-committed to the Revision Committee to look at the form of calling down the Spirit, to take on board what is now Prayer G, and to provide an 'inter-active' Prayer. In November 1999, at the Second Revision Stage, the first two of these requirements were met, and the third became the subject of a further round of revision, till a text of Prayer H was accepted without amendment at the General Synod in February 2000. All eight prayers which follow were incorporated into the text of the whole Communion service and were overwhelmingly approved on 1 March 2000 to be in use for an open-ended period beginning on Advent Sunday 2000. The 'sample' text was then published on 6 April 2000.

What then is the purpose of a eucharistic prayer? At first sight, the answer is obvious—it is to 'give thanks' (the meaning of 'eucharist'). It is highlighted in the third versicle and response of the opening dialogue:

Let us give thanks to the Lord our God.
It is right to give thanks and praise.

At the Last Supper Jesus gave thanks to God in relation to the bread first and again at the end of the meal in relation to the cup. From very early times it appears that the church has brought the two elements together and uttered a single thanksgiving, viewing it as one of the two major actions of the eucharist (the other being distribution) which we do 'in remembrance of' our Lord Jesus.[14] The thanksgiving has included a remembrance of the mighty acts of God, particularly in Christ, but also an account of the institution and a petition for the bread and wine to 'be' the body and blood of Christ. In the West, this petition traditionally came before the narrative of institution and was viewed by Roman Catholics as being answered in the miraculous change which occurred in the elements when, during the narrative, the priest uttered Jesus' words 'This is my body...this is my blood.' Thus in the Middle Ages more and more ceremonial accompanied those words, ceremonial which was revived in Anglicanism by the anglo-catholic movement in the nineteenth century—and is often still around.

But Anglicanism outside England has also in various times and places adopted an 'Eastern' position for the petition, and this has usually taken the form of ask-

---

13   For the texts of these six prayers and an account of them, see Colin Buchanan and Trevor Lloyd (eds), *Six Eucharistic Prayers as Proposed in 1996* (Grove Worship booklet W136, 1996).

14   The other (lesser) two, making up Dix' 'four-action shape,' are the first (taking) and the third (breaking the bread).

ing the Father to send the Spirit to make the action effectual. In the actual Eastern Orthodox rites this was known as the 'epiclesis,' a term which has now been adopted in Western discussion also, being used sometimes even for prayers which do not mention the Spirit, but include a 'petition for consecration.' The main difficulty with such prayers for Western anglo-catholics has lain not in their text but in their position within the eucharistic prayer—for the conventional Eastern position is subsequent to the narrative of institution and, if it is to be taken seriously as petition, it seems to set aside the narrative of institution as not having consecrated the bread and wine. Prayers D, F, G and H in differing ways exhibit this shape in the new Order, but in fact it does not seem to have caused much reaction.[15]

Evangelicals have been more concerned about the form of such a petition, and in particular have been unhappy with any text which suggested that the Spirit was being called upon the elements, rather than on the action or on the people. There was a tussle about this in Synod as the prayers were going through, and the resultant texts do invoke the Spirit in broad terms but are unspecific about the action of the Spirit in relation to the actual elements! There is good hope they will satisfy all schools of thought.[16]

The broad position taken in worldwide Anglicanism at least since Lambeth 1958 is that 'consecration' is by thanksgiving, and the whole thanksgiving prayer must be viewed as consecrating. There is then no one 'moment' when the transformation happens and when weighty ceremonial accoutrements are appropriate. It will be noted that, in all the modern language revisions of the eucharist in the Church of England since Series 3 in 1971, all reference to manual acts to accompany the narrative of institution has been dropped from the texts, and the 'taking' of the bread and cup comes properly before the thanksgiving starts.

15 A very comprehensive essay in defence of this position for the invoking of the Spirit (a structure of the prayer which the Liturgical Commission started in the early 1990s to call 'The Trinitarian Structure') was produced by Thomas Talley, the American Episcopalian liturgical scholar, in David R Holeton (ed), *Revising the Eucharist: Groundwork for the Anglican Communion* (Grove Joint Liturgical Study 27, 1994).
16 See Colin Buchanan, *Eucharistic Consecration* (Grove Worship booklet W148, 1998).

The Congregational Parts: The Text

The **Eucharistic Prayer**

An authorized Eucharistic Prayer is used. The president says

The Lord be with you   *or*   The Lord is here.
and also with you.   **His Spirit is with us.**

Lift up your hearts.
We lift them to the Lord.

Let us give thanks to the Lord our God.
It is right to give thanks and praise.

The president praises God for his mighty acts and all respond
Holy, holy, holy Lord...[Blessed is he...Hosanna in the highest].

The president recalls the Last Supper, and one of these acclamations may be used

[Great is the mystery of faith:]   [Praise to you, Lord Jesus:]
Christ has died: **Dying you destroyed our death,**
Christ is risen: **rising you restored our life;**
Christ will come again.   **Lord Jesus, come in glory.**

[Christ is the bread of life:]   [Jesus Christ is Lord:]
When we eat this bread and   **Lord, by your cross and resurrection**
    drink this cup,   **you have set us free.**
we proclaim your death, Lord Jesus, **You are the Saviour of the world.**
    until you come in glory.

The Prayer continues and leads into the doxology, to which all respond boldly **Amen.**

In Prayer A this response may be used **To you be glory and praise for ever.**

and the Prayer ends   **Blessing and honour and glory and power**
                             be yours for ever and ever. Amen.

In Prayer D these words are used   This is his/our story.
                             This is our song:
                             Hosanna in the highest.

and the Prayer ends   **Blessing and honour and glory and power**
                             be yours for ever and ever. Amen.

In Prayer F these responses may   **Amen. Lord, we believe!**
be used   **Amen. Come, Lord Jesus!**
                             Amen. Come, Holy Spirit!

In Prayer G the Prayer ends   **Blessing and honour and glory and power**
                             be yours for ever and ever. Amen.

For responses to Prayer H see page 56

3B

The Congregational Parts: Commentary

The page facing this reproduces pages 28–29 in the official published text of Order One. It is designed to help the congregational response, with all those responses for the first seven Prayers (*ie* nos A–G) being set out in bold type in full, with the relevant cue words to trigger the response also being shown in some cases. Whilst the full text is not provided at this point, yet the structure of those first seven starts to emerge from the responses, and the layout of them is not far from the ground-plan of the four Prayers in Rite A in the *ASB*. The text of the third response in the opening dialogue is changed from previous Church of England texts: '**It is right to give him thanks and praise**' became in the international texts '**...to give our thanks and praise,**' but is here '**...to give thanks and praise.**'[17]

There is no given cue word for the Sanctus ('**Holy, holy, holy**'), but the climax of the Preface in the first seven Prayers leaves worshippers in little doubt, and those reading this page alone (on which see below) should have little difficulty.

The four different forms for the acclamations are a major expansion of the text in Rite A, where only the first of these four occurs. With a choice of four, this Order needs the cue words spoken, and the worshippers' subconscious will learn to respond with the right words to each cue. In Prayers A and E the acclamations now come after the anamnesis, one paragraph later than in Rite A (or in B, C and G here). Purists are critical of responses which, in a Prayer addressed to the Father, here address the Son, and that may affect the choice of acclamations made.

The assumption about the climax of the Prayer is that the doxology will lead to an obvious place for the response '**Amen.**' However, those who only use this page need to read on without delaying, as it is revealed lower down that Prayers A, D and G actually end with the longer congregational doxology '**Blessing and honour...**' (the cues to which have again to be discerned as they are uttered).

It gets harder after this, as the specific responses for each Prayer include some for which no cue is given, and, in the case of Prayer F, three different one-line responses come in sequence at unknown intervals.[18] These puzzles would make most worshippers who wish to engage with the Prayer to want the whole text in front of them. But in fact this page does not tell how many Eucharistic Prayers there are, nor where they are to be found in the Order, nor the cues they give for some of the responses. They are but seven pages further on, but worshippers *must not find them* (except Prayer H). The full book may be better.

---

17   The ELLC text was moving gently away from referring to God as 'he' and 'him,' not in an exhaustive way, but so as to reduce the number of masculine pronouns used for God. Our own Revision Committee clearly thought that ELLC's replacement possessive adjective was not as felicitous as a straight omission of both pronoun and adjective.

18   On inspection the first is used four times, the second once, the third twice. But would you guess it?

4A

Prayers A, B and C: Texts

[Prayer A follows the First Eucharistic Prayer in Rite A except as shown[19]]
It is indeed right...through Jesus Christ your Son our Lord.
The following may be omitted if a short Proper preface is used.
For he is your living Word...formed us in your own image.
[To you be glory and praise for ever.]
Through him you have freed us from the slavery of sin,
giving him to be born of a woman and...exalted him to your right hand on high.
[To you be glory and praise for ever.]
Through him you have sent upon us...a people for your own possession.
[To you be glory and praise for ever.]
Short proper Preface, when appropriate.
Therefore with angels and archangels...praising you and *saying*:
Holy, holy, holy Lord...[Blessed is he...Hosanna in the highest.]
Accept our praises, heavenly Father...may be to us his body and his blood;
who in the same night...given for you; do this in remembrance of me.
[To you be glory and praise for ever.]
In the same way, after supper...as often as you drink it, in remembrance of me.
[To you be glory and praise for ever.]
Therefore, heavenly Father, we remember...and glorious ascension;
we look for the coming of your kingdom,
and with this bread and this cup
we make the memorial of Christ your Son our Lord.
   [Cued acclamations as on page 10 above]
Accept through him...the body of your Son, Jesus Christ our Lord.
[To you be glory and praise for ever.]
Through him, and with him, and in him...in songs of everlasting praise:
Blessing and honour...for ever and ever. Amen.

[Prayer B follows the Third Eucharistic Prayer in Rite A except as shown.]
Father, we give you thanks and praise...to be our Saviour.
By the power of the Holy Spirit he took flesh...won for you a holy people.
Short Proper Preface, when appropriate
Therefore with angels and archangels...praising you and saying:
Holy, holy, holy Lord...[Blessed is he...Hosanna in the highest.]
Lord, you are holy indeed...to us the body and blood of our Lord Jesus Christ;
who in the same night...given for you; do this in remembrance of me.
In the same way, after supper...as often as you drink it, in remembrance of me.
   [Cued acclamations as on page 10 above]

---

19 The opening dialogue for each Prayer is on page 10 above, and the full text of congregational responses also.

12

And so, Father, calling to mind his death on the cross,
his perfect sacrifice made once for the sins of the whole world;
rejoicing in his mighty resurrection and glorious ascension,
and looking for his coming in glory,
we celebrate this memorial of our redemption.
As we offer you this our sacrifice of praise and thanksgiving,
we bring before you this bread and this cup
and we thank you for counting us worthy
to stand in your presence and serve you.
Send the Holy Spirit on your people...for ever and ever. **Amen.**

[Prayer C follows the Fourth Eucharistic Prayer in Rite A except as shown.]
It is indeed right...through Jesus Christ our Lord;
Proper Preface, when appropriate
[Or, when there is no Proper Preface:
For he is our great high priest...a royal priesthood to you, our God and Father.]
Therefore with angels and archangels...praising you and saying:
Holy, holy, holy Lord...[Blessed is he...Hosanna in the highest.]
All glory be to you...memory of his precious death until he comes again.
Hear us, merciful Father... partakers of his most blessed body and blood;
Who in the same night...given for you; do this in remembrance of me.
In the same way, after supper...as often as you drink it, in remembrance of me.
        [Cued acclamations as on page 10 above]
Therefore, Lord and heavenly Father...sacrifice of praise and thanksgiving.
Grant that by his merits and death...grace and heavenly blessing;
through Jesus Christ our Lord; by whom...for ever and ever. **Amen.**

4B

Prayers A, B and C: Commentary

Prayer A: The origins of the First Eucharistic Prayer in Rite A are described above on pages 6–7. In all those years the chief debate was about the anamnesis—the paragraph stating what 'we do' in response to Jesus' command. In Prayer A the expanded acclamations (on which see page 11) come one paragraph lower than they do in Rite A, and thus the 'Therefore, heavenly Father...' does respond immediately to Jesus' command.

That said, we note other minor ways in which this Prayer has altered the Rite A one. In the Preface 'born as man' has not surprisingly (nor controversially) become 'born of a woman' (see Gal 4.4). Then, as the Second Eucharistic Prayer of Rite A has perished, some of its distinctive features have been fitted into this Prayer A. One is its provision to drop the centre of the main Preface when a short Proper

Preface is used, and that adds to the flexibility here. On the other hand, two features of the original Series 2 anamnesis, features viewed as provisional at the time and replaced in Series 3, have crept back in from the Second Prayer (which was Series 2 modernized), and have displaced better texts. We now look 'for the coming of your kingdom' (which is not *too* bad[20]), but have lost 'we celebrate his one perfect sacrifice' (to which in Rite A the following '...this our sacrifice of thanks and praise' provided a literary foil and an exact theological balance). Instead we have the 1967 jejune and opaque 'we make the memorial of Christ your Son our Lord.' It is a small blemish we could have done without.

The new interspersed response can well step up the mood of joyous acclaim of the Lord who died and rose for us, and this matches the triumphant congregational doxology which concludes the Prayer. But, as shown on page 11 above, there are no cue words for it, and only those with a full text before them (or much past experience) can be expected to acclaim confidently.

Prayer B: The Third Eucharistic Prayer arrived in Rite A in 1978 by a side-wind through a submission to the Revision Committee of Synod made by Brian Brindley and Roger Beckwith. The two had done a curious deal, in which Roger Beckwith would support the Hippolytan-type prayer for Brian Brindley's sake, if he could have a modernized 1662 for his own sake.[21] However, the 1978–1979 Revision Committee took the Hippolytan Prayer (which also owed quite a bit to Roman Catholic Prayer II) and re-touched it. Thus, for instance, in the 'second epiclesis,' the Father was now asked to send the Spirit upon his people rather than on the elements. The upshot was a new Prayer, which has had very wide use, and been much appreciated. Here the Prayer remains as in 1980 as far as the anamnesis (where it modifies 'the sins of all *men*'); but the next paragraph has been shortened by two lines, with a skilful invisible mending that few will spot.

Prayer C: This Prayer, virtually identical to the Fourth Prayer in Rite A, is a direct descendant of 1662 and of Cranmer's 1552, concentrating narrowly but profoundly upon the death of Christ. It retains the fully 'receptionist' epiclesis which is characteristic of Cranmer (and, being in 1662, is the standard of doctrinal orthodoxy for the Church of England)—'Grant that...we receiving these gifts of your creation, this bread and this wine... may be partakers...' The second half of the Prayer has a simple anamnesis and then draws upon the 1662 post-communion 'prayer of oblation' and, in a carefully revised form avoiding actual self-oblation, brings that back into the Eucharistic Prayer itself (as in 1549 and the 'Interim Rite').

---

20 There was a story about how this first came into Series 2. See Michael De-la-Noy, *Mervyn Stockwood* (Mowbray, 1996) p 145 and Colin Buchanan in General Synod in July 1999.

21 It was an asymmetrical deal, as the Revision Committee had *already* agreed to provide the modernized 1662 as an option, and Brian Brindley, as a member of the Committee, already knew this when he struck the two-faced bargain with his partner.

Prayer D: The Text

The Lord be with you   *or*   The Lord is here
and also with you.   **His Spirit is with us.**

Lift up your hearts.
We lift them to the Lord.

Let us give thanks to the Lord our God
It is right to give thanks and praise.

Almighty God, good Father to us all,
your face is turned towards your world.
In love you gave us Jesus your Son
to rescue us from sin and death.
Your Word goes out to call us home
    to the city where angels sing your praise.
We join with them in heaven's song:

Holy, holy, holy Lord,
God of power and might,
heaven and earth are full of your glory.
Hosanna in the highest.
[Blessed is he who comes in the name of the Lord.
Hosanna in the highest.]

Father of all, we give you thanks
    for every gift that comes from heaven.

To the darkness Jesus came as your light.
With signs of faith and words of hope
he touched untouchables with love and washed the guilty clean.

This is his story.
This is our song:
Hosanna in the highest.

The crowds came out to see your Son,
    yet at the end they turned on him.
On the night he was betrayed
he came to table with his friends
    to celebrate the freedom of your people.

This is his story.
This is our song:
Hosanna in the highest.

Jesus blessed you, Father, for the food;
he took bread, gave thanks, broke it and said:
This is my body, given for you all.
Jesus then gave thanks for the wine,
took the cup, gave it and said:
This is my blood, shed for you all
    for the forgiveness of sins,
Do this in remembrance of me.

This is our story.
This is our song:
Hosanna in the highest.

Therefore, Father, with this bread and this cup
we celebrate the cross
on which he died to set us free.
Defying death he rose again
and is alive with you to plead for us and all the world.

This is our story.
This is our song:
Hosanna in the highest.

Send your Spirit on us now
that by these gifts we may feed on Christ
    with opened eyes and hearts on fire.

May we and all who share this food offer
    ourselves to live for you
and be welcomed at your feast in heaven
    where all creation worships you.
Father, Son and Holy Spirit.
Blessing and honour and glory and power
be yours for ever and ever. Amen.

5B
Prayer D: Commentary

Prayer D is a totally new Prayer, produced by the Liturgical Commission in the wake of the defeat of the six in 1996.[22] Its style and language are meant to be accessible for children, but it is not labelled as specifically a 'children's eucharistic prayer.' One interesting touch is the phrase 'good Father'—a protection and corrective for those whose experience of earthly fatherhood has not been good.

The key to understanding its working is the word 'narrative.' The Prayer is meant to be less abstract in its language than some tend to be, and instead it focuses very firmly upon the story of salvation. This is why it has its repeated cue and response 'This is his/our story. **This is our song.**' The president needs to engage with this underlying purpose and to articulate the Prayer in such a way that the narrative flow emerges clearly. The Prayer does not lend itself to ceremonial but it does lend itself to drama.

One way suggested for evidencing the drama is to lift the bread and cup at appropriate intervals—not for theological reasons but as part of the dramatic praying of the Prayer. Other gestures—such as hands raised high in the air in celebration, or in openness to receiving the Spirit—may also fit the drama well. Visual imagery, added by projection (using PowerPoint or even slides on an OHP) can enhance the verbal imagery of the Prayer also.

There is a strong emphasis on the love of God reaching out to the errant sinner, especially in the early part of the Prayer. The theme of the heavenly banquet recurs, as well as the expression of grace in the earthly life of Jesus. Within all the themes, however, the responses gave the Revision Committee the greatest concern. During the time they were before the Committee they were changed—and then changed back again. Was the echo of the old hymn, 'Blessed Assurance,' too low-brow? Or was it in fact so little known in a younger generation that it would not be recognized anyway—which would minimize any temptation to burst into low-brow song? The texts survived, and now time will tell whether the echoes affect people's engagement with the flow of the Prayer and its responses. Apparently there are already different contemporary musical settings being composed...

In use the cue line 'This is his/our story' may be said by other voices, and one of us (Charles Read) used it during the trial period with a group of children, so triggering the full congregational response—and it heightens the drama.[23] This is the key to the best use of it—it needs a proactive congregation and a mood of celebration, and it does not lend itself to the quiet midweek or early Sunday morning event so easily.

---

22 Rumour connects its origins with a consultation between Bishop James Jones, when he was Bishop of Hull, and one of his own children.

23 The role of children is increased if a lead-in by children is used with preparation prayer 8 from page 146.

6A

Prayer E: Text

[Opening dialogue as on page 10]

Here follows an extended preface (pages 148 and 154–83) or the following
Father, you made the world and love your creation.
You gave your Son Jesus Christ to be our Saviour.
His dying and rising have set us free from sin and death.
And so we gladly thank you,
with saints and angels praising you, and *saying:*
Holy, holy, holy Lord...[...Hosanna in the highest.]

We praise and bless you, loving Father,
through Jesus Christ, our Lord;
and as we obey his command,
send your Holy Spirit
that broken bread and wine outpoured
may be for us the body and blood of your dear Son.

On the night before he died he had supper with his friends,
and, taking bread, he praised you.
He broke the bread, gave it to them and said:
Take, eat; this is my body which is given for you;
do this in remembrance of me.

When supper was ended he took the cup of wine.
Again he praised you, gave it to them and said:
Drink this, all of you;
this is my blood of the new covenant,
which is shed for you and for many for the forgiveness of sins.
Do this, as often as you drink it, in remembrance of me.

So, Father, we remember all that Jesus did,
in him we plead with confidence his sacrifice
        made once for all upon the cross.

Bringing before you the bread of life and cup of salvation,
we proclaim his death and resurrection
until he comes in glory.

One of these four acclamations is used   ***[Cued acclamations as on page 10]***

Lord of all life,
help us to work together for that day
when your kingdom comes
and justice and mercy will be seen in all the earth.

Look with favour on your people,
gather us in your loving arms
and bring us with (*N and*) all the saints
to be with you for ever at your table in heaven.

Through Christ, and with Christ, and in Christ,
in the unity of the Holy Spirit,
all honour and glory are yours, O loving Father,
for ever and ever. **Amen.**

6B
Prayer E: Commentary

This a Prayer of some brevity—but is longer if use is made of the extended prefaces. It has only the traditional responses, though, as with several others, including the greater choice now of acclamations. These acclamations, as in Prayer A, now come one paragraph beyond the narrative of institution, instead of immediately on its close, thus allowing the anamnesis ('So, Father, we remember...') to respond in direct sequence to Jesus' command 'Do this in remembrance of me.' The Prayer is conservative in providing an epiclesis in the 'Western' position, *prior* to the narrative of institution. It thus would credibly allow that the narrative's provision at the dominical words identifies focussed points of consecration, as has been characteristic of 'Western' catholics.[24]

The epiclesis itself went through various draftings, as the Commission had drafted a text which invoked the Spirit on the gifts as well as on the people. The Synod desired the Revision Committee to reconsider this feature, and they returned with the slightly vague, but wholly inclusive, text 'send your Holy Spirit, that...'[25] This most obviously implies an invocation of the Spirit on the whole sacramental action, on the thanksgiving and on the giving and receiving of the elements. However, people are free to read it with whatever nuances they wish.

Because of the great range of possible prefaces this Prayer can always be made seasonal and show great variety round the year. But its unchanging latter half gives a glimpsed vision of God's kingdom of justice and mercy, and a directing of the worshippers towards that kingdom through participation in communion.

---

24 The present authors would still urge that such identification of the 'moments' of consecration is contrary
   to the spirit of the Prayer, which, like all the others, is drafted for 'consecration by thanksgiving.' But the
   shape of this one does not absolutely rule out people's slanting of the Prayer towards those 'moments.'
25 A similar change had been made in the earlier Revision Committee to a similar 1996 Prayer, but the
   Liturgical Commission ignored this when drafting new texts, and the Revision Committee then denied
   that the step had ever been taken until shown the 1996 text—and then they followed suit.

Prayer F: Text

The Lord be with you	*or*	The Lord is here.
and also with you.		**His Spirit is with us.**

Lift up your hearts.
We lift them to the Lord.

Let us give thanks to the Lord our God.
It is right to give thanks and praise.

You are worthy of our thanks and praise
Lord God of truth,
for by the breath of your mouth
you have spoken your Word,
and all things have come into being.

You fashioned us in your image
and placed us in the garden of your delight.
Though we chose the path of rebellion
you would not abandon your own.

Again and again you drew us into your covenant of grace.
You gave your people the Law and taught us by your prophets
to look for your reign of justice, mercy and peace.

As we watch for the signs of your kingdom on earth,
we echo the song of the angels in heaven,
evermore praising you and *saying*:
Holy, holy, holy Lord…[…Hosanna in the highest.]

Lord God, you are the most holy one,
enthroned in splendour and light,
yet in the coming of your Son Jesus Christ
you reveal the power of your love
made perfect in our human weakness.
[Amen. Lord, we believe!]

Embracing our humanity,
Jesus showed us the way of salvation;
loving us to the end
he gave himself to death for us;
dying for his own,
he sets us free from the bonds of sin,
that we might rise and reign with him in glory.
[Amen. Lord, we believe!]

On the night he gave up himself for us all
he took bread and gave you thanks;
he broke it and gave it to his disciples, saying:
Take, eat, this is my body which is given for you;
do this in remembrance of me.
[Amen. Lord, we believe!]

In the same way, after supper
he took the cup and gave you thanks;
he gave it to them, saying:
Drink this, all of you; this is my blood of the new covenant
which is shed for you and for many for the forgiveness of sins.
Do this, as often as you drink it, in remembrance of me.
[Amen. Lord, we believe!]

Therefore we proclaim the death that he suffered on the cross,
we celebrate his resurrection, his bursting from the tomb,
we rejoice that he reigns at your right hand on high
and we long for his coming in glory.
[Amen. Come, Lord Jesus!]

As we recall the one, perfect sacrifice of our redemption,
Father, by your Holy Spirit let these gifts of your creation
be for us the body and blood of our Lord Jesus Christ;
form us into the likeness of Christ
and make us a perfect offering in your sight.
[Amen. Come, Holy Spirit!]

Look with favour on your people
and in your mercy hear the cry of our hearts.
Bless the earth,
heal the sick,
let the oppressed go free
and fill your Church with power from on high.
[Amen. Come, Holy Spirit!]

Gather your people from the ends of the earth
to feast with (*N and*) all your saints
at the table of your kingdom,
where the new creation is brought to perfection
in Jesus Christ our Lord;

by whom and with whom, and in whom,
in the unity of the Holy Spirit,
all honour and glory be yours, almighty Father,
for ever and ever. **Amen.**

7B
Prayer F: Commentary

This Prayer is explicitly based on a Prayer by Basil of Caesarea, though the Liturgical Commission worked over the original very fully.[26] Structurally, it is fairly conventional, with the (unchanging) Preface focussing on the history of salvation and stressing the covenant love of God in the face of our infidelity ('Again and again you drew us into the covenant of grace'). The narrative of institution is set in the context of Jesus' self-offering, which is itself seen in incarnational terms ('Embracing our humanity'). The epiclesis (in the 'Eastern' position, and reinforced if the acclamation 'Come, Holy Spirit' is used) is a prayer that we might grow into the likeness of Christ as the fruits of communion. We ask that we may thus be formed by God's grace into a 'perfect offering.' The old protest against self-oblation in the eucharistic prayer, arising from the hint of Pelagianism in it, is charmed away by the perspectives now in place—firstly that it is by God's grace that we are able to offer ourselves to him, and secondly that, as that grace is conveyed through reception, it is a responsive (and logically post-communion) sacrifice of ourselves we are seeking to offer, though mentioned in the eucharistic prayer.

The three brief intercessions in the last section of the Prayer are an almost unique example in the Church of England of an echo of the long tradition (of both Rome and the East) of weaving intercessions into this prayer. The intercessions were separated from the eucharistic prayer in 1552, and became a substantial feature of the ante-communion, rather than being found solely in the eucharistic prayer. But the provision of eight prayers enables a frontier to be pushed out.

The optional acclamations by their very presence or absence give two totally different styles to the Prayer. If they are not used, then it becomes a monologue from the Sanctus and Benedictus onwards, and, in effect, leaves the congregation more passive than in any other Prayer of the eight. If the acclamations are used, then, granted that the people are dependent upon a lead from the front (see page 11 above), it looks as though some second string (a deacon in circles that take the liturgical deacon seriously) must trigger the congregation's part—presumably by uttering the loud 'Amen' which begins it. The congregation will have to know that the three variants come in a ratio of 4-1-2, or they will be clashing with each other in the responses. It will not be easy for the newcomer to respond confidently even when a cueing 'Amen' has triggered it.

Nevertheless, we can imagine (and do so from some experience) that the pneumatic strand in the Church of England will love this Prayer. Its rich imagery may not make it first choice in every parish, but many will give it a good innings.

---

26   At the first Revision Stage, there was a footnote to '[**Amen. Lord, we believe**]': 'These optional acclamations echo the style of those in the Liturgy of St Basil, and might—especially when sung—be led by a deacon or minister other than the president... Other acclamations may be used.'

8A
Prayer G: Text

[Opening dialogue as on page 10]

Blessed are you, Lord God,
our light and our salvation;
to you be glory and praise for ever.

From the beginning you have created all things
and all your works echo the silent music of your praise.
In the fullness of time you made us in your image,
the crown of all creation.

You give us breath and speech, that with angels and archangels
and all the powers of heaven
we may find a voice to sing your praise:
Holy, holy, holy Lord...[...Hosanna in the Highest.]

How wonderful the work of your hands, O Lord.
as a mother tenderly gathers her children,
you embraced a people as your own.
When they turned away and rebelled
your love remained steadfast.

From them you raised up Jesus our Saviour, born of Mary,
to be the living bread,
in whom all our hungers are satisfied.

He offered his life for sinners,
and with a love stronger than death
he opened wide his arms on the cross.

On the night before he died,
he came to supper with his friends
and, taking bread, he gave you thanks.
He broke it and gave it to them, saying:
Take, eat; this is my body which is given for you;
do this in remembrance of me.

At the end of supper, taking the cup of wine,
he gave you thanks, and said:
Drink this, all of you; this is my blood of the new covenant,
which is shed for you and for many for the forgiveness of sins.
Do this as often as you drink it, in remembrance of me.

One of the following is used
   [Cued acclamations as on page 10 above]

Father, we plead with confidence
his sacrifice made once for all upon the cross;
we remember his dying and rising in glory,
and we rejoice that he intercedes for us at your right hand.

Pour out your Holy Spirit as we bring before you
these gifts of your creation;
may they be for us the body and blood of your dear Son.

as we eat and drink these holy things in your presence,
form us into the likeness of Christ,
and build us into a living temple to your glory.

[Remember, Lord, your Church in every land.
Reveal her unity, guard her faith,
and preserve her in peace...]

Bring us at the last with (*N* and) all the saints
to the vision of that eternal splendour
for which you have created us;
through Jesus Christ, our Lord,
by whom, with whom, and in whom,
with all who stand before you in earth and heaven,
we worship you, Father almighty, in songs of everlasting praise:
Blessing and honour...Amen.

8B
Prayer G: Commentary

This Prayer came into the set of eight Eucharistic Prayers at a very late stage. It has its origins in a text composed by the Roman Catholic International Committee for English in the Liturgy (ICEL) in 1986, and a text very like it was among the six proposed to General Synod in February 1996 and then defeated there—which is why it was not among the new texts proposed by the Commission in 1998. The Bishop of Oxford sent it in to the Revision Committee, which did not accept it but pointedly printed its text in its report; the Bishop had another go, asking the Synod that its first half might become a further Preface for Prayer F. The Committee this time proposed the whole Prayer, the Synod hardly debated it, and so it entered the package as Prayer G in November 1999.

The reasons for including the Prayer lie in the imagery which is distinctive to it, imagery which is evocative and memorable and affects our understanding of God. Several phrases need special highlighting.

'...all your works echo the silent music of your praise'

'Silent music' is paradoxical enough—let alone that which gives an 'echo'! The imagery echoes our experience of God who is simultaneously surrounded in the silent awe of all creation in his presence—and in the praises, shouted and sung, of the company of heaven and earth which worships him without ceasing. Can both points be made in one phrase? John of the Cross in the sixteenth century framed the paradox and we draw gratefully upon his writing.

'...the crown of all creation'

We are used to eucharistic prayers which acknowledge either that God created us or that he created the universe. But this rare form neatly and evocatively gives us our place in the creation, in the purposes of God and through his handiwork. Subsequent thoughts arise: as the crown of creation it is our task to praise our creator—and, a little later, as the crown of creation it is all the more appalling that we turn away from our creator.

'...as a mother tenderly gathers her children
you embraced a people as your own.'

These lines have sometimes been thought to promote the idea of God being a Mother. However, they draw simply on a comparison attributing to God the protective love of a mother, very mildly using maternal imagery. The source is Jesus' words over Jerusalem 'How often I would have gathered you to me as a hen gathers her chickens under her wing' (Luke 13.34). They were the foundation for the famous meditative prayer of St Anselm, *A Prayer to St Paul*, in the eleventh century and have inspired highly creative ways of praying since.

'...form us into the likeness of Christ,
and build us into a living temple to your glory.'

Both these metaphors stem from the letter to the Ephesians and both have wound their way into Anglican liturgical devotion through being included in the Second Eucharistic Prayer of Rite A in the ASB—they were much loved there but that Prayer has been dropped in the taking of the other three through into this Order. 'Living temple' is particularly the theme of Eph 2.20-21, whilst being formed into Christ's likeness (through an astonishing process of bonding and maturing) comes in Eph 4.13-16.

All this imagery is packed tight, overlapping with other imagery (as in the last extract above), and wrestling in the minds of worshippers with the normal demands of the Communion service for our understanding of its significance. This does suggest that, in congregations where it is used, it cannot simply fulfil a tokenist role about our readiness for feminine imagery, but actually needs slow and meditative ways of forming part of our devotional make-up. It is a prayer to be taught, to be savoured, to be absorbed—and thus to be truly prayed.

Prayer H: Text

[Opening dialogue as on page 10]

It is right to praise you, Father, Lord of all creation;
in your love you made us for yourself.
When we turned away
you did not reject us
but came to meet us in your Son.
**You embraced us as your children
and welcomed us to sit and eat with you.**

In Christ, you shared our life.
that we might live in him and he in us.
**He opened his arms of love upon the cross
and made for all the perfect sacrifice for sin.**

On the night he was betrayed,
at supper with his friends
he took bread, and gave you thanks;
he broke it, and gave it to them saying:
Take, eat; this is my body which is given for you;
do this in remembrance of me.
**Father, we do this in remembrance of him:
his body is the bread of life.**

At the end of supper, taking a cup of wine
he gave you thanks, and said:
Drink this, all of you; this is my blood of the new covenant
which is shed for you for the forgiveness of sins;
do this in remembrance of me.
**Father, we do this in remembrance of him:
his blood is shed for all.**

As we proclaim his death and celebrate his rising in glory,
send your Holy Spirit that this bread and wine
may be to us the body and blood of your dear Son.
**As we eat and drink these holy gifts,
so make us one in Christ, our risen Lord.**

With your whole church throughout the world
we offer you this sacrifice of praise,
and lift our voice to join the eternal song of heaven:
**Holy, holy, holy Lord,
God of power and might.
Heaven and earth are full of your glory.
Hosanna in the highest!**

Prayer H: Commentary

A truly interactive eucharistic prayer is not new. *A Eucharist for the Seventies*, by Trevor Lloyd and Christopher Byworth (printed three times 1968 to 1970) provided a lead to which the Grove Worship Series is in succession.[27] The Bishops turned down the idea in 1978; tendencies of this sort in 'Rite C' in *Patterns for Worship* in 1989 were aborted when those texts failed to get anywhere;[28] and the 1998–2000 Revision Committee began by rejecting submissions for such a prayer. So Prayer H came as the floor of Synod drove the platform at the First Revision Stage in July 1999. The Revision Committee then circulated a draft, received submissions, and re-drafted the text for the Second Revision Stage in November 1999. There it ran into procedural complexities, and was withdrawn. The Revision Committee received further submissions, met yet again, and proposed a new draft to Synod in February 2000, who quickly accepted it.

The Prayer's controlling characteristic is to be 'inter-active'—president and people forming the Prayer by alternation, so that the people's part contributes to the developing story of the Prayer (not, as in others, being simply endorsements of the presidential part). The Prayer is also the shortest of the eight, and is quite child-friendly, but these are incidental features, and were not part of its drafters' terms of reference. Trial and error in the new field meant that the two-line response by the people would be standard, with a constant address to the Father.

Within its short text there are still depths of meaning, subtleties of imagery. The Bishop of St Albans, introducing it for the last time in Synod, said: "'In your love you made us for yourself" may set up resonances with St Augustine's phrase, "You made us for yourself and our hearts are restless till they find their rest in you", or [another instance is] George Herbert's poem, "Love bade me welcome" which is hinted at in the phrase "and welcomed us to sit and eat with you."' But that same section, with its 'came to meet us in your Son' also derives, like David Frost's post-communion prayer, from the story of the Prodigal Son.

Even in such a short compass, there is an embryonic anamnesis and a sufficient (Eastern-position!) epiclesis. There is a Synod-tossed problem about a final 'Amen.'[29] But for a Committee-written eucharistic prayer to meet profound theological needs on the one hand, and to be both true to the tradition and yet wholly innovative on the other—that is an astonishing prescription, which the Prayer meets amazingly well. It needs to be said briskly—in each part.

---

27 So of course is Prayer H itself, as *A Eucharist for the Seventies* provided the Sanctus as a climax of praise.
28 At a late stage in the process of providing the six prayers which were defeated in February 1996, Prayer 6 emerged as a principled retouching, by the then Revision Committee, of the First Eucharistic Prayer of Rite A slightly shortened, slightly restructured, but re-allocated to be highly interactive—see COB and Trevor Lloyd (eds), *Six Eucharistic Prayers as Proposed in 1996* (Grove Worship Booklet W 136) pp 22–23.
29 See General Synod *Report of Proceedings* for 28 February 2000.

Appendix:
'Table Prayers' and Other Related Texts

The actual Prayers A–H are not the full story, and appendixes to the Orders contain three different kinds of auxiliary materials relating to the Eucharistic Prayers.

i) Seasonal Prefaces

These are short prefaces (of the conventional 'And now we give you thanks...' sort) to go with Prayers A, B and C, along with 'extended prefaces' to go with Prayers A, B and E. Prayers D, F, G and H do not admit of seasonal variation. Curiously there is one seasonal extended preface tucked in among other 'supplementary texts' (p 148). Whilst extended prefaces greatly increase the sense of a long presidential monologue, they are also rich with scriptural content, genuinely giving a different flavour or emphasis to particular Sundays and seasons.

ii) Prayers at the Preparation of the Table

These are a mixed collection—1 to 3 being overtly about money, 4 to 8 being wholly about the sacrament, and 9 to 12 being more general in their application. Number 4 bears upon our present purpose, as it is a variant on the post-Vatican II Roman 'offertory prayers.' Because these prayers have previously included the words '...this bread to offer...this wine to offer...' they were not explicitly printed in Rite A, though the response '**Blessed be God for ever**' was there and dropped a broad hint about their fittingness. Now a new text is offered:

'...this bread to set before you...this wine to set before you...'

This was Michael Vasey's idea for a way of not saying 'offer' and yet having a text which could be printed. It is not so clear that 'set before' is either free of the 'offering' connotations or likely to be used in this eclectic translation.[30] And such prayer is anticipating the eucharistic prayer and may itself be a mini-canon!

Prayers 5 to 8 here all have a particular history, 5 in the Church of South India, 6 in the Didache of the second century AD, 7 again in the genius of Michael Vasey, and 8 in the overture to the 'Alternative Eucharistic Prayer A' of Rite C in 1989. Each has riches—though each delays the eucharistic action.

iii) Supplementary Consecration

In Order One supplementary consecration is effected by the use of a formula, carried forward from Rite A. This includes part of the narrative of institution and retains 'by the power of your Holy Spirit' but still in principle extends the context of consecration by referring back to the single thanksgiving already offered, rather than by stark repetition of Jesus' words of institution (in 1662 style).

---

30 Limited experience so far (May 2000) would suggest that those who like the Roman prayers go on using them as they always have; and those who do not like them have not adopted the Vasey redraft.